The Moment I Looked Back

Role of God in Our Lives...Knowledge Is Power

The Moment I Looked Back

Role of God in Our Lives...Knowledge Is Power

Virginia Lee Edge

ARPress
45 Dan Road Suite 5
Canton MA 02021

Hotline: 1(888) 821-0229
Fax: 1(508) 545-7580

Ordering Information:
Quantity sales. Special discounts are available on quantity purchases by corporations, associations, and others. For details, contact the publisher at the address above.

Printed in the United States of America.
ISBN-13:   Paperback   979-8-89330-591-3
                eBook   979-8-89330-592-0

Library of Congress Control Number: 2024902602

PROLOGUE

We knew God was carrying us

To keep looking up. God is always there (never look back). Endow me with your Spirit that I can rise higher and higher.

THE LORD, THY GOD, TELLS US TO TEACH OUR CHILDREN AND KEEP HIS COMMANDMENT ALWAYS. THAT IT WILL BE WELL WITH OUR CHILDREN AND WITH US FOREVER BUT, ARE WE DOING WHAT'S WRITTEN IN THE WORD OF GOD? LET'S SEE HOW WE ARE DOING!

Contents

Purpose

Before you can find meaning, you first must discover and identify with your self-identity (your personality)! We all have questions in our heads; is God real for us? Have we ever seen him (True) but, we are here on this earth for a purpose in God's plan for our lives. To understand the meaning of our existence, we need to understand God's plan for our lives.

God's words are evident in the Bible. But how do we study when we do not have an encouraging support system involved in the home. To provide a caring, stable teaching environment to study. Generally, both parents are out of the house working to provide for their families. How do we learn the Bible truth, for the answers to guide us to God's living Word?

This ingenious work of art God gave to humankind to learn of Him, Man is wasting for the lack of knowledge of God's Word. We need to set aside time to teach our children God's word. That's the answer!

God has a master plan for every human being living on this earth; He gave Man free well. But Man needs to understand, with free will, we still need to ask God for guidance!

God has given us the Bible as an instruction manual to help guide and teach us. But Man, thought-out the ages has strayed away from God's Word which gives life, wisdom, and understanding.

Man can't go through Life without God's teaching and guidance in His Word. We must be stewards of God's Word to become superior in understanding through the study of God's Word.

1 Corinthians 4:15 For though ye have ten thousand instructors in Christ, yet not many fathers: for in Christ Jesus, I have begotten you through the gospel.

1 Corinthians 4: 16 Wherefore I beseech you, be ye followers of me.

God is letting all know loud and clear through the reading of His Word: His people (Children) need to learn of him.

God knows everything we do; He has an army of angels that form hedges of protection around our lives if we just believe in His Word; learn to follow the commandments of God.

We just need to call on Him and read His Word (the Bible), or we tie God's hands thinking we can go through Life without Him, the devil is waiting to steal, kill, and destroy humankind.

God will remove his hands over your life, and you will learn the lesson the hard way. But, once you utterly understand what God wants for your life, you will not forget.

God is talking to everybody that will hear His Word; do you think you can find your way in Life without God's help?

Did you forget something? God created this earth and everything in it. He even created good and evil? If you just read Isaiah 45:6 and Isaiah 45:7 it says as follows:

Isaiah 45: 6 That they may know from the rising of the sun, and from the west, that there is none beside me. I am the Lord, and there is none else.

Isaiah 45: 7 I form the light, and create darkness: I make peace, and create evil: I the Lord do all these things.

God gave everything to a man. Then Man lost everything though disobedient by eating of the forbidden fruit in the Garden of Eden (the Paradise God set for us). Why are we not curious enough to read the Bible and start in Genesis and ask God for wisdom and understanding.

Dominion is ours, and that's the secret for us from God, and we lost everything through our disobedience.

Then God gave us Jesus the Christ to die for our sins, to resurrect us again.

God gave us the Holy Spirit, the Spirit is pure, but the soul can still become corrupt, which is within Man's inherent nature. Now that we have the Holy Spirit in us, it's continually guiding and teaching. But, if we do not keep God's words in our hearts, mind, and soul, we can still go astray, and the devil is waiting.

Since most people are emotionally blind and not educated with God's Words of Wisdom and insight, they cannot see the forest for the trees.

The Bible says in: Proverbs 9:9 Give instruction to a wise man, and he will be yet wiser: teach a just man, and he will increase in learning.

God talks to us every day, appealing to his children, that we need to know of Him. People's moods are changing, and everything around us is being affected by our disobedience. Are you asking yourselves how to stop this bleeding before it is too late? The answer is in front of us; all we need to do is start reading God's Word and cry out for His help (show me, God, show me). If you ask with a pure heart, God will immediately answer you.

Some friends of yours might just ask you to go to church with them the following Sunday, or it may be a church program scheduled in Town that your friends can attend with you. When you cry out for help, God will put someone or something in your life to help you. God always answers!

It doesn't cost you anything; just reach out to start reading the Bible and ask God for his help, wisdom, and understanding.

God will show you what you're looking for as long as you keep your focus on Him and ask.

God's love is a beautiful experience when you take the time to learn of HIM in Jesus' name!

It says in Proverbs 22:6 (KJV)

Train up a child in the way he should go, and when he is old, he will not depart from it.

It says in Deuteronomy 11:2 (KJV)

And know ye this day: for I speak not with your children which have not known, and which have not seen the chastisement of the Lord your God, his greatness, his mighty hand, and his stretched- out arm.

WOW

The Creation of the world in Genesis: AND GOD SAID LET THERE BE, AND it WAS!

Here we are, let's see if you can find your way. And not be blind in understanding! You lose what you don't use if you think you're smart, you're not. The principle of power is having greater Faith in God for understanding His wisdom.

God speaks to your Spirit, your Spirit speaks to your mind, and your soul speaks to your mouth. And your mouth speaks to the universe. When you are looking for a miracle, talk with your mouth with no doubt in your heart, and the answers will come.

When your mind speaks the same language as God through your Spirit, nothing will be impossible.

In the mouth, the tongue words are so powerful, never send the devil negative signals from your mouth (watch your tongue).

Matthew 12:28 But if I cast out devils by the Spirit of God, then the Kingdom of God is come unto you.

King James Version: Psalms "Cast Thy Burden Upon the Lord"

Psalm 55:1 Give ear to my Prayer, O God; and hide not thyself from my supplication.

I am pleading to God in Prayer.

Psalm 55:2 Attend unto me, hear me: I mourn in my complaint, and make a noise.

Psalm 55:3 Because of the voice of the enemy, because of the oppression of the wicked: for they cast iniquity upon me, and in wrath they hate me.

Do you have to ask yourselves, why do people just hate? Men hate because they do not understand the intellectual functions of life and God's unconditional love.

CHAPTER 2

Equality

Equality means the state of being equal, especially in status, rights, and opportunities. Something is very confusing when relating to the Bible; there is no mention of racial equality in the Bible.

God made Man, a rainbow society, of beautifully blended colors, and God loves us all. For there is no respect of persons with God: See KJV in Romans 2:11

Romans 2: 11 For there is no respect of persons with God.

In Man's blind pursuit of racial equality, one study below answers this question?

Research by Kellogg School of Management entitled "In Blind Pursuit of Racial Equality?"

As quoted from the reading: "Researchers sought to determine the impact of colorblindness on elementary school students' capacity to recognize racially motivated incidents and subsequently report them to facilitate adult intervention."

The researchers were Evan P. Apfelbaum of the Kellogg School of Management at Northwestern University, Kristin Pauker of Stanford University, Samuel R. Sommers, and Nalini Ambady of Tuft University.

The article will appear in a forthcoming issue of Psychological Science, a journal of the Association for Psychological Science.

"Inmany ways,the logic behind colorblindness is understandable, that downplaying racial distinctions should limit the potential for bias.

"We see this ideology prominently displayed in many social settings, from the strategies people use to avoid discussion of race in interracial interactions.

To broader efforts at education reform in which administrators challenged with managing diversity among school districts and within classrooms," said Apfelbaum, visiting assistant professor of management and organizations at the Kellogg School."

Proverbs 9:10 The fear of the Lord is the beginning of wisdom: and the knowledge of the holy is understanding.

"Perhaps most of us are alarmingly blind well educated, but no wisdom and understanding of what God appears to be telling us!

Because we did not form this earth or set the sun, moon, clouds, and stars in the sky, a man can't explain this at all. We do not have that power.

Man can use insulting words to quiet the Spirit and fool the soul of another man or group. A form of mental judo on the mind to control another individual or group that does not think for themselves.

If a man does not read and educate himself and learn the words of God, how will Man learn to have a thinking mind that can ask questions? Man will not gain this way by not thinking for himself.

"Despite such discouraging signs, however, our study suggests that colorblindness may not reduce bias as much as it adjusts the lens through the bias".

"In Blind Pursuit of Increasing Man's Education, Knowledge and Wisdom of God" is to Man, an invaluable piece of his life's walk with God. "

Do we need a popular vote to be at peace with each other's thoughts; do we have to be puppets on a string and hide our true meaning to please others!

Why not just love one another, and let God be our guide since racial inequality is Man's form of controlling and corrupting our society.

If, for example, we leave our children alone and teach them to love one another, they will not have the bias in their hearts against racial indifferences.

It is the adults that spread this type of poison an imbalance, from generation to generation. Hate only grows when you feed it.

Equality and a tenacious titillating spirit give a dreamer growing room to lift his or her courage. God always lets you choose the way you wish to go (He gives free will).

Quotes: By William Arthur Ward:

"The pessimist complains about the wind; the optimist expects it to change; the realist adjusts the sails. Gratitude can transform common days into thanksgivings, turn routine jobs into joy, and change ordinary opportunities into blessings".

"The mediocre teacher tells" "The good teacher explains"

"The great teacher inspires." Quotes: By Marcus Aurelius:

"You have power over your mind – not outside events.

Realize this, and you will find strength".

"Everything we hear is an opinion, not a fact."

"Everything we see is a perspective, not the truth."

"The universe is change; our life is what our thoughts make it."

"Waste no more time arguing about what a good man should be. Be one

CHAPTER 3

Mental and Physical Understanding

How can we measure Man's real understanding when his knowledge of differences is his reality?

Because Man's (male and female) reality of others theoretically, surrounds his perception of the environment he's living in!

And our perception is our reality if we have a consciousness. It's all about how Man perceives the world surrounding him By collecting data from U.S. citizens (adults) to view their moral differences and reasoning by asking questions such as:

"Can objective morality exist without God." "Moral argument, Does God exist."

Does 2+2 equal four (4)

Turn on the T.V. and listen to the hostile rhetoric that fills the ears of society today.

Are we subjected to the theories and objective thoughts of other people that appear to be more persuasive in their speech to control?

I wonder, for example, does the economic policies of our society keep one's mind floating in the wrong direction day by day.

Aimlessly, trying to find the meaning of just being, or why is hate what it is today, and why is it snowballing to the point of no return?

God help us to understand this cruelty of such evil that has befallen us and stop it in its tracks.

Do we believe in the fundamentals of Human Rights (Intelligence Exist)? Yes, we do.

We need to Increase Man's awareness in education and knowledge of the laws that exist.

We have many challenges in our society, with the voting rights not being equal, minimum wage $8.56 an hour, overpopulation, gender inequality.

Anyone can access your private information without written approval; hackers are savvy when it comes to obtaining information. And we are slowly polluting our water, soil, and the air we breathe with unknown chemicals today? The wealth of our Nation takes precedence over what is going on; you can't clean up the Nation if the pursuit is after the mighty dollar.

Eventually, everyone's life will suffer because of human immorality and universal exposure to the toxic waste products in our environment, which alters every plant, animal, and human species on this earth's DNA.

Then you have the problem with People's fundamental human rights being mistreated within certain ethnic groups because of being different for no other reason.

Then you have some people no longer happy with the way their bodies look. They will have surgery to change the way they look, nose job, lips enlarged, breast enlarged, butt enlarged, just to name a few. But a lot of these people seem to be very angry with themselves.

Mysticism is creeping into society at an incredibly fast pace, disrupting families, and provoking increase hate, among others.

Unique strength is needed to confront people that are hurting. This hate is real, and prejudice is a sickness that's raising its head again, like when blacks were in Slavered. And Hitler tried to exterminate all the Jews.

It looks like if you do not fit into the status quo, you do not belong. But you should never let someone else's hate destroy your joy for life. Get up off your butt and get an education and improve your status in life.

CHAPTER 4

Disruptive Thought's

When a man's words are arranged (written) or spoken in a provocative manner that disrupts your thoughts, that does not mean the delivery is wrong; it means your understanding is not at that level of that person's real belief.

When disruptive thoughts start to show themselves as intrusive thoughts; the person could be exemplifying an Obsessive- Compulsive- Disorder (OCD); that could relate to a stressful situation.

This stressful situation, exemplified by laughter and smiling all the time to cover up their true feelings, shows that the person cannot handle what's going on in their life.

Mood swings may be noticed when they cannot have their way. They do not like to hear what to do, which is interesting enough to know.

Direct criticism is not accepted, even if the logic is correct and honorable!

Take the Bible; Man will never understand; he will continue to interpret and extrapolate out of the Bible what is a more straightforward message to follow. Instead of reading the Bible in it's entirely to study and learn.

But it says God's thoughts will always be above Man's understanding (God wants us to read His Word and learn of Him and not extract the topics we do not like).

Why do we drown in distaste (displaced anger) and sleep in the absence of control?

"In Freudian Psychology, displacement is an unconscious defense mechanism whereby the mind substitutes either a new aim or a new object for goals felt in their original form to be dangerous or unacceptable."

Displaced anger directed onto another target; that is how some people handle their feeling. Some people are silent and disengaged, or some people act out and can become very abusive, physically, or verbally.

We are drowning in life because we have taken on too much. Take a breather ask God for help because you will never have control in the beginning; that is why stress builds up.

Learn how to love yourself and let God take the anchor of your ship (your life).

It says in Hebrews 13:5 (KJV)

Let your conversation be without covetousness; and be content with such things as ye have: for he hath said: I will never leave thee, nor forsake thee.

We cannot walk until someone shows us how. We will never know what the absence of control is or even true love until it is in our hearts, heads, and rooted in our souls (it is not explained, the journey gives the experience)!

The journey is necessary for life as we grow in Wisdom and Understanding to bear the burdens that come up throughout life.

Enjoy this walk, it will get comfortable if you do not lose your focus, and God is in front.

It says in Proverbs 12:11 (KJV)

He that tilleth his land shall be satisfied with bread: but he that followeth vain persons are void of understanding.

We tend to forget, if we do not understand our soulish realm, we will not understand the spiritual realm, which is uplifting, and encourage others through Prayer.

God formed Man's body from the dust of the earth; God breathed into Man and gave Man a living soul.

Let everyone that has breath Praise the Lord!

Man's body and soul were perfect before Satan fooled Man into eating the forbidden fruit of the garden.

The soul and the body changed because the soul now knew evil, but the Spirit didn't change. Because once we are born again, we receive a perfect sense that is dealing with a non-perfect soul.

Through Jesus Christ, God came to renew us and restore our souls. Jesus came to this earth through miracle childbirth.

God the Father, Son, and Holy Spirit and God said in Genesis: Genesis 1:26 And God said, Let us make Man in our image, after our likeness: and let them have dominion over the fish of the sea, and over the fowl of the air, and over the cattle, and overall the earth, and over every creeping thing that creepeth upon the earth.

Humankind messed up by touching the forbidden fruit of the garden! The devil gained access to our five senses, ears, eyes, nose, taste, touch, because of our disobedience.

And Satan used all five gates of our senses to defile and corrupt our soul (all five of the gates are open, and sin walked in).

IN JESUS NAME – GOD HELP US ALL

It says in: Psalm 150: 1 (KJV)

Praise ye the Lord, Praise God in his sanctuary: praise him in the firmament of his power.

WOW

God's sanctuary is wherever we experience God's Love.It says in Matthew 6:6 (KJV)

But thou, when thou prayest, enter into thy closet, and when thou hast shut thy door, pray to thy father which is in secret; and thy father which seeth in secret shall reward thee openly.

LOVE SONG

Love Song: The Excerpt from the Song Poet: By Kao Kalia Yang I learned how to sing love songs long before I learned how to love. I knew the love of a mother, of brothers and sisters, and the continual turn that good friends take through years of being together.

There is more. You must read this book by Kao Kalia Yan

CHAPTER 5

Youmustbelieveinyourself!

When you fall, you get up, that is what you did when you put on your first pair of roller skates, right!

Didn't it feel good to know you were able to get back up and learn to skate? That is what it means never to give up, you will get it right, and you will discover a powerful lesson.

Here is my poem about: The Tree that Wise Man can see By Virginia Lee Edge

The tree informs us about our life. The tree is God's gift to Man.

It moves with the wind, rain, and storms but never gives up. Because it is planted solidly in the ground as God would have it be.

The tree knows it is around for a season, and besides, it helps other trees to continue to grow.

A tree's life can be hundreds of years or cut down in a twinkle of an eye.

Their roots are planted firmly in the ground (boy did God do a great job); they speak a language to the air and mother earth that no man understands. Their roots and branches understand Man's life.

The tree knows how to communicate and provide for each following tree, even when the time to be cut down, it gives root for another tree and man's shelter. But Man is still not wise enough to understand.

The tree tries to show Man how he is to live.

The tree looks into the woods; a wise man stops and looks around and up and down at the beauty of the trees for the first time.

The wise man now notices the different colors and understands what God's meaning is!

That beauty and love have always been in all of us unconditionally from birth, but we never stop to learn of everything God has created and given to us. God Said Let There Be; everything was fashioned just on God's Word to infinity (with no end).

The wise man can now see how he has lost his way by not learning the love of the trees and the little things in life that go with it.

Never be too busy to notice the poetry and rhythm of the trees that God has given us; it is something extraordinary.

The trees know; God has given Man the power. Like a tree, it knows how to use all the power that God has given it.

Why has not Man learned how to use his power, the same as the tree it knows what it stands for? The tree is what wise men can see; the tree was first in God's garden; now, the trees are all around us, and they are all exceptional.

CHAPTER 6

MyVoiceisanInvisibleVapor

Your voice is a trusted friend (an invisible floating vapor), but your tongue can be your worst enemy if you let it. Let us learn to speak life into our family, friends, and other people that cross our daily paths.

It says in Psalm 34:13 (KJV)

Keep thy tongue from evil, and thy lips from speaking guile. It says in Psalm 34:1 (KJV)

I will bless the Lord at all times: his praise shall continually be in my mouth.

My voice is an invisible floating vapor; one day, I will pass from one world (God's Earth) to the next and be with God.

But, before that time comes, we have a lot of work that needs to be done, winning a generation of people back to the Lord our God (Praises are going up, and Blessings are coming down) AMEN to the believer in God's Word!

When I say enjoy this long train ride (this journey), I mean enjoy your journey through life.

You will have one chance to get your life right, get on and off as many stations that you can.

And teach as many people that you can; of God's Word (be a blessing to as many as you can).

Each station you get off will be different, and you will equip yourself to handlings of each station in life. Get on God's train. He has a lot of stops for you to make along this journey.

We have a lot of people to meet to spread the Lord God's Love and His Word, all praises to God in Jesus's mighty name.

My voice is an invisible floating vapor, we wish to make a difference if we just touch a few people in life, and they affect a few more, and so on. Our living and journey in life would not have been in vain.

My voice is an invisible floating vapor. We mean to touch many lives through our nature of being vigilant with everyone and anything that crosses our path.

Man, sometimes does not always understand the nature of unconditional love (there are no strings attached).

If only you truly knew God, His Word is the nature (the life, the seed) you are His Word, his unconditional love given freely with one touch.

In one touch, we train up our children in the way they are to go, and let's pray it's with God's blessing (your contact is the journey in the life of the child).

God gives all of us understanding, a measure of Faith (trials in life are necessary to help us grow), and a little intestinal fortitude to deal with all the other things that will pop up along the way. Still, we must always learn to put God first in all that we do. We must discuss every detail with God and get His stamp of approval.

Never take it upon yourselves to be the leader of your destiny; God leads you to follow!

My voice is an invisible vapor. Your struggle is not your own; when God leads, there is no confusion.

God has been talking to everyone all over the world lately, but we are hard of hearing.

He is letting us know. We are destroying ourselves for the lack of His (God's) knowledge. God left the Bible for us to read for our improvement for body, mind, and Spirit (Wake up everybody).

Quotes: By Arvo Part

"The Human voice is the most perfect instrument of all."

"I had to get rid of everything unnecessary to save myself." "A room without books is like a body without a soul."

Quotes: By Maya Angelou

"Words mean more than on paper. It takes the human voice to infuse them with deeper meaning."

"Nothing will work unless you do."

"If you don't like something, change it. If you can't change it, change your attitude."

CHAPTER 7

ParentsareaBlessingfromGod

My voice is an invisible floating vapor. Parents are a blessing from God, and we are to be a blessing to our children from one generation to the next. We are to plant in our children God's Word; His Word is the seed. His name will travel with strength from one generation to the next generation to every part of the world.

As the waters flow around the world, so will the seed of God's Word!

Yeshua (Jesus) in the Jewish Bible (Jewish Messiah) from the beginning Jesus is God.

KJV Matthew 1:23

Behold a Virgin shall be with child and shall bring forth a Son, and They Shall Call His Name EMMANUEL which being interpreted God with us.

My voice is an invisible vapor. We are getting to be an apathetic world of people God is not pleased, wake up people, look around you. So what is your relationship with yourself going to be, think of these words?

Our world is imploding on itself and just incinerating before our eyes more ways than one. We need to continue praying for the family's unity to remain stable, think of these words!

My voice is an invisible vapor, as God's children, we do not know how to call on Him. We must have one unitary voice in Prayer to God and stop and drop to our knees and fast and pray for the entire world to come back to knowing God (there is a strong need around this world for God's help).

My voice is a vapor; every one of us has been called by God to do the work of God. Serve God every day of our lives, and this is the easy job anyone could ever have working for the Lord God. When you move to the Lord's side, you will find life more abundant.

Remember, our battle is not with the Lord. There are other giants in our lives, and we do not have to fight these giants. Like David and Goliath, David used a slingshot with a stone to slay the giant Goliath. But David knew God, and he released Faith by releasing the stone into Gods' hand, and the giant fell.

We need to have Faith more abundantly to release our stones into God's hand. Most people today are keeping their life's problems inside; these problems are heavy burdens to carry.

It takes great Faith, and God's Love and your words are spirits, speak to the Lord thy God with a pure heart. And see if he doesn't answer you. He will!

Man can overcome the evils of the devil in their lives, first by Jesus Christ, who died for our sins, and by the words of God. That's why, if you're fighting the devil, use God's words on him. The devil isn't afraid of Man. He fears the power of God's Word.

And, when God has a child of His that can use His words against the devil, God will be right there for you.

Isaiah 54:17 No weapon that is formed against thee shall prosper, and every tongue that shall rise against thee in judgment thou shalt condemn. This is the heritage of the servants of the Lord, and their righteousness is of me, saith the Lord.

The power of the tongue is mighty, and Lord God's words are potent. Read these words that come from the Bible that is for your use today.

Isaiah 55: The Messiah's Invitation to the world

55:1 Ho, everyone that is thirsteth, come ye to the waters, and he that hath no money; come ye, buy, and eat: yea, come, buy wine and milk without money and price.

Isaiah 55: The Messiah's Invitation to the World

55:2 Wherefore do ye spend money for that which is not bread? And your labour for that which satisfieth not? Hearken diligently unto me, and eat ye that which is good, and let your soul delight itself in fatness.

55:3 Incline your ear, and come unto me: hear, and your soul shall live: and I will make an everlasting covenant with you, even the sure mercies of David.

55:4 Behold, I have given him for a witness to the people, a leader, and commander to the people.

55:5 Behold, thou shalt call a nation that thou knowest not, and nations that knew not thee shall run unto thee because of the Lord thy God, and for the Holy One of Israel; for he hath glorified thee. 55:6 Seek ye the Lord while he may be found, call ye upon him while he is near:

55:7 Let the wicked forsake his way, and the unrighteous man his thoughts: and let him return unto the Lord, and he will have mercy upon him: and to our God, for he will abundantly pardon.

55:8 For my thoughts are not your thoughts, neither are your ways my ways, saith the Lord.

55:9 For as the heavens are higher than the earth, so are my ways higher than your ways and my thoughts than your thoughts.

Isaiah 55: The Messiah's Invitation to the World

55:10 For as the rain cometh down, and the snow from heaven, and returned not thither, but watereth the earth, and maketh it bring forth and bud, that it may give seed to the sower, and bread to the eater:

55:11 So shall my Word be that goeth forth out of my mouth: it shall not return unto me void, but it shall accomplish that which I please, and it shall prosper in the thing whereto I sent it.

55::12 For ye shall go out with joy and be led forth with Peace: the mountains and the hills shall break forth before you into singing, and all the trees of the field shall clap their hands.

55:13 Instead of the thorn shall come up the fir tree, and instead of the brier shall come up the myrtle tree: and it shall be to the Lord for a name, for an everlasting sign that shall not be cut off.

Isaiah Chapter 55: 1- 13, in Isaiah, has a way of talking to your Spirit, you can still make a covenant with God, and you are always to seek him. And God's words never come back void when he speaks. There is so much to learn from this chapter.

Personal Pride:

Always take the long-short way and not the short, long way because you need to learn, and it takes time to learn. That's why you should not take shortcuts first.

If you take the short, long way, you'll have roadblocks with no understanding and no answers, vision, or value in your life.

Always take the long-short way; this will give you God's world; it gives you time to learn and understand.

A tenacious spirit gives Man room for growth, even if Man doesn't start on a positive foot. A titillating sense gives Man some growing room to lift himself. God (Jesus) lets you choose the way you wish to go, free will.

How can a man find his way, without the real help of the Lord, our God?

We built the house but not in a day; first, the foundation must be poured and set, then the walls go up. God (Jesus) will show you! Dream big, the driving forces are to invest in yourself, be consistent, not giving up, no matter what.

Your season is right around the corner, perform like you are the King, and never give in to your fears because fear is not of God.

Have peace in your hearts, measure the changes you need to do. Man cannot measure your vision or the distance you will travel to get to where you want to go.

CHAPTER 8

Everythingisstartingto Change

My voice is an invisible vapor lookout world. We are becoming a perverse world of people. We not only fight among ourselves, but we are also struggling with God. His Word is not our guide any longer, so we try and do all things ourselves without any guidance. Sorry People, this is all wrong.

My voice is an invisible vapor. Have you noticed the weather lately violent hurricanes, tornadoes, turbulent storms, earthquakes, tsunamis, sinkholes, and uncontrollable fires across the earth? Which has been wiping out whole towns of people across the states and several countries, every year it gets worse, killing thousands of people with no recourse. Look at buildings today falling and killing thousands of people is this not a sign of man's destructive behavior?

Who is responsible for all this destructiveness? Is it Man's evil doings?

As soon as the government steps in to fix the problem, we have another catastrophic insult to our environment.

There are not enough human resources with skills to immediately take on the needs and requests of the millions of people (and where is all this money coming from to handle this)!

My voice is an invisible vapor before we know it, we will all feel the devastation by these natural disasters; what will we do then?

I bet everyone will drop to their knees, fast, and pray. Our lives are not void of pain and suffering. We are not in a room by ourselves; we are God's children.

The world (the people) has a different name for our God, but we all have just one creator call Him what you will let us stop the fighting. Our Genre will be To Join Hands and Made Peace.

My voice is an invisible vapor. Once we disagree to agree, then yes, we will move forward obviously with dignity and style to turn our countries and Nations around. No one person is an expert on any joint venture. It takes a team to make things work in life.

We must remember God does not have to learn anything, He is the Master, and we are the clay.

My voice is an invisible vapor, never concern yourself with someone putting you down, and never concern yourself with someone throwing stones because those stones have a habit of turning around and coming back to the sender.

Seek the Kingdom of God to serve Him, and all your ways will be prosperous in God's eyes. Your mind feeds on what you hear, see, and think. By this observation, train your mind to be positive by changing your mindset. Prosperity is not just money; don't be conformed to the system of the world. Ask God to open the eyes of your mind that you can see and understand.

Just remember worry is a soul problem, so if you are going to pray, don't worry. But, if you continue to suffer, do not pray, since you are not leaving your concerns in God's hands.

My voice is an invisible vapor, any man that thinks he's more subservient than anyone else is fooling himself. You don't have to push anyone out of your way. You know who you are, and you don't have to prove your point if you know where you stand.

Shine your shoes for yourself and not for anyone else. They will stay shined longer.

A thinking mind gives birth to all its thoughts and helps you to integrate and solve problems. Failure is a part of success; you will learn from it. Just seek God; he will meet your needs.

Your voice is an invisible vapor. Wisdom is the smartest appetizer on your plate; it gives you all the dressing that you need to deal with anything.

A saying: The closes mouth to your ears is your mouth. So, guard it carefully; negative words feed negative feedback, positive words give positive input, and unbelievable strength!

Do not complain or murmur; give God (Jesus) in Prayer all your concerns, and He will provide you with the spiritual understanding that you deserve.

My voice is an invisible vapor. Never let another person wash your face with negative words. The dirt they lay for you; they will pick it up along the way. Let God handle that truculent personality. It's not yours to bear!

My voice is not a vapor, a story about a dog that Man can relate to today. A dog had a bone. He went across the bridge to walk alongside the riverbank. He suddenly looked in the water and saw another dog with a Bigger bone (it was his reflection). When he opened his mouth to reach for the Bigger bone, his bone fell in the water.

The story says to be happy with what you have. The grass will always look greener on the other side. And you have no way of knowing how it got that way.

Keep on writing until you get your thoughts correctly down and together on paper. One day it will all be more transparent, and others will understand more clearly as they follow you down this road with you and God's understanding. God will always send you someone to help you and be a blessing or help to someone else.

Keep writing, start typing, and the more you let your thoughts flow, the better you will get.

Ask God (Jesus) for understanding, wisdom, and knowledge. To do the things you want to do, to build a life of opportunity for yourself. Blessings come along, the more you put God (Jesus) first in your life, keep praising God in Jesus' name, walk by Faith and not by sight.

Remember, you will never lose if you don't give up. You need to build a bridge to cross, start slowly, and grow. If a mountain does not move, then you must pass it.

Experiences change your life.

The nature of experience is life itself that will change your life as you continue to live and grow emotionally, mentally, and physically. Our life is fluid, mixed with elements, sadness, evil, loneliness, profound visions, and growing Faith.

Why do we long for things we cannot have? Is it because we don't have a real understanding of life itself? Our experience and growth are not in our knowing. Our growth is in our understanding of what life is all about.

CHAPTER 9

When Man Struggles

My voice is an invisible vapor. Hear this when a man struggles to see the light in his eye; he is not at the level of real understanding of God.

God says, take a glimpse into His Word and read of Him! God will validate everything you read; just ask Him.

Just remember certain things in our lives will not move by Prayer unless you fast, and you pray. Something happens to a person when he or she fasts and prays, they humble their souls, and God sends the instructions and the direction they need to take.

My voice is an invisible vapor: My Quotes: by Virginia Lee Edge

Hunger hates waste.

Be a blessing to someone else.

Love is not blind, but you sure need sunshades. Mind your business.

My color doesn't define me; my response does. Keep your business to yourself.

A relationship with unconditional love can endure all things.

Freely gift another through your giving.

You need to be responsible for yourself.

Life is a recipe that can be found in any Bible because God (Jesus) never changes.

If you think you're so much better than someone else, then you're overdressed.

Your clock can never buy my time, so just be patient.

Never measure your life by other people's opinion of you, since their light can't see how bright yours is shining already.

Put money away for a rainy day, because it's sure to come.

Teach your children how to hold on and win in any storm; it will not last long.

Always go to God (Jesus) in Prayer. He is your rock.

Always give Praise and Thanksgiving to God (Jesus). He will always answer.

What travels around the world, every day, and does not answer to any man, or pays for anything? The answer is MONEY!

What is the most incredible luxury in Life that God has given us on this earth? The answer is: TO HAVE A GREAT FRIEND!

What dictionary should you be reading THE BIBLE OF Wisdom?

Always rejoice in the Lord, by Prayer, let your requests be made known. The Peace of God shall keep your heart and mind through Christ Jesus.

CHAPTER 10

Without a Voice

My voice is an invisible vapor; how can someone learn without a sound? They know in the silence, which can be very therapeutic for the individual and gives that person a different perspective on life. Speech in your presence alone (that of a Baby); can be uncomfortable if the silence is genuinely not understood.

It's just better to listen.

The tongue is a lethal weapon that should be tamed, but the conversation lets you know the measure of a man now that you hear and see.

My eyes have seen my ears have heard the measure of Man's heart I believe I have listened to, and I now know better out of the mouth spills what's truly is in the heart of a man.

Power awareness WOW.

I need your Spirit, God, endow me with your Spirit that I can rise higher and Higher and not be afraid.

God endows me with your Spirit that I can rise above all that confronts me daily in life.

I am so lost even though I know you are there with me every day of my life. You see, Lord God, I am caught up in Man's daily living of what we are all responsible for.; why is this that man's regular schedule so programs us.

I see so many young people like me trying to figure out what they want out of life, but they do not have a clue of how to move forward in their lives.

Every day you move forward without your Father God, you get deeper and deeper into this world of despair (discouragement, unhappiness, hopelessness). What more can I tell you?

When you are in this state of hopelessness, you need to sit back and go over your life alone with your Father God, call on Him and relax and let your Spirit from God make the connection with you (not you with Him) he will answer you in the still of your soul.

Stillness will come over you, your feelings of life will feel more natural, and you will lose the struggle that you feel in your body and mind.

You will learn to live with greater Peace of mind. The college that you worked so hard for in high school has come to fruition because you persevered and maintained your focus.

Quote: by Virginia Lee Edge

Learn from people who are willing to make you better.

Never put off today what you may not be able to do tomorrow.

As a young person, can you make plans for your life? Yes, you can! But never forget to confide in God in Prayer for guidance, wisdom, and understanding. And God will guide your every step of the way. God is the only one that knows your heart and what road you need to take in life. If you ask God, he will not let you take this walk alone. Talk to God in the Holy Spirit and let your Spirit know what you want because God communicates with us in His Spirit.

And as you acquire knowledge, you need to continue to apply yourself.

Start going to the library to get books to read and keep up with all your studying (just apply yourself).

Knowledge comes by applying yourself and studying as you continue to increase your intuitive understanding of reading literary books that make you dream and open your mind to factual information, which will enrich your mind with more knowledge making you even smarted. Possibilities for you are great to advance into any educational field in your lifetime. Because of becoming an independent thinker. Who has entertained different areas of knowledge that have integrated your reasoning and thinking to solve and question the why of everything!

My voice is not a vapor. I have no power unless I use what God gave me. I have no value if I don't know who I am, and Jesus is my source. And self-worth comes from God-Christ Jesus, and God Christ Jesus must be the most crucial person in your life.

The Word of God is the tithe; it's our seed; the name is everything. The Word was in the beginning; the Word was God. He made all things. Without God, nothing would exist; the physicists will search the universe and never find God.

Man will preach the Word of God as he interprets and applies the message, but we are to seek God, who is our source for clarity and understanding because God's thoughts and knowledge are much higher than Man.

Everything from the Kingdom of God is a seed. Put Faith in the Word of God.

Mark 4:14 The sower soweth the Word.

Root the Word of God deep in your Spirit and heart, do not be afraid, and only believe God is. AMEN

The Bible talks about the love, sex of a man and women; this Bible addresses their lives and the commandments they are to follow. And it does not speak to Man about a perverted Love for one another.

What man does not understand is the different experiences that change your life if you are not in God's word. The nature of this experience is life itself. You are growing emotionally, mentally, and physically. And our lives are fluid, mixed with elements of sadness, evil, loneliness, profound visions, and increasing Faith.

Why do we long for the things we cannot have or afford? It's because we don't have a real understanding of life itself. Our experience and growth are not in our knowing; our expansion is in our understanding of what life is all about.

First, we are not our own. We are only on this earth for a short time, which is only a moment in God's time and not in ours. Yes, just a moment, yesterday is today, and tomorrow will be tomorrow. What you had yesterday is no longer what you have today, not confusing, it's real, and you need to understand the Psychology of Man's needs. Man needs to understand his beginning to appreciate his ending.

Because of Man's miss understanding of life, he fears the ending and the fear of the unknown. Our creator is God, Wow!! We need to set our minds on God in Jesus's Name!! God will teach us daily about life and why we are here on this earth. Is this something to speculate? Yes!

God created a family, husband, wife, and children. Children are gifts to their parents, and parents are to train them up in the likeness of God (Jesus).

Parents are to be a Blessing to their children for generations to come. We plant God's words (His seeds of life) in our children to strengthen their souls and mind since God's Spirit within Man is incorruptible. The Spirit is free from corruption. Only souls and thoughts can corrupt.

Here is another thing to search ourselves, a lot of us truly do not think we have a voice any longer. We are walking robots we believe everything we listen to on television.

My voice is not a vapor I will write this as a fiction tale. We have a pandemic Covid-19 virus that shot up in years. In the beginning, I am talking to God now: would it have been wise God for the Health

Industry and the governing bodies to come straight out and tell all the people we have a major virus crisis. And God while they were on TV, should they have said, clean your house, apartment, phone with disinfection spray(like Lysol), purchase gloves (boxes)for cleaning.

Buy a face mask that covers your nose to your mouth (boxes), hand washing front to back with soap, and water a most, this is for every human being, on this earth (if you have dogs, cats keep them clean).

Because this is a contagious process we are facing. All stores that sell merchandise will be stocked with the necessary disinfection supplies, masks, gloves as needed. Make sure that you have all the necessary food items and toiletries etc.

And now God, that the Health and governing bodies have addressed the general public on TV News of the health crisis, what is next.

Next to the Health advisory department and governing body will let everyone know they have a new experimental vaccine, God I will use the names of the experimental vaccine I saw in the papers:

Manufacturer: Pfizer, Inc., and BioNTech Names: BNT162b2 Type of Vaccine: mRNA Number of shots: 2 shots, 21 days apart

How Given: Shot in the muscle of the upper arm Does Not Contain: Eggs, preservatives, latex, metals But here is the list of ingredients it contains:

Active ingredient: Nucleoside-modified mRNA encoding the viral spike (S) glycoprotein of SARS-CoV-2

Inactive ingredients: 2{(polyethylene glycol (PEG))-2000}- N,N-distearoyl-sn-glycero-3-phosphocholine. Cholesterol.

(4-hydroxybutyl)azanediyl)bis(hexane-6,1diyl)bis(2-hexyldecanoate)

Sodium Chloride, Monobasic potassium phosphate, Potassium chloride, Dibasic sodium phosphate dihydrate, Sucrose.

Inventor: Dr. Ugur Sahn and Dr. Ozlem Turect Then there is the Moderna (mRNA)

Then there is Johnson & Johnson Janssen (viral vector),

These two vaccines would be interesting to look up and the ingredients added

"The inventors of the Pfizer Vaccine"

" Is a Husband- and –Wife Team Behind the Leading Vaccine to Solve Covid-19, Dr. Ugur Sahn and Dr. Ozlem Tureci, the couple who founded BioN Tech."

"The Husband-and-Wife Team founded the German company BioNTech. Founded by the above two scientists, has teamed up with Pfizer on a vaccine that was found to be more than 90 percent effective to treat Covid-19."

Some history on the two doctors, Dr. Sahn who is Turkish, was born in Iskenderun Turkey. When he was 4 years old his family moved to Cologne Germany. Dr. Tureci was born in

Germany, the daughter of a Turkish physician who immigrated from Istanbul.

This is why we must read….GOD wants us to know! Quote by Maya Angelou

"If I am not good to myself, how can I expect anyone else to be good to me?"

So what is your relationship going to be with yourself?

This is not confusing it is addressed this way to make you think about these things. God wants us to grow in His words and know where we stand at all times in our lives.

Quote by Maya Angelou

"Stand up straight and realize who you are, that you tower over your circumstances."

"I'm a phenomenally, Phenomenal woman, that's me."

"People will forget what you said, people will forget what you did, but people will never forget how you made them feel."

"You can't use up creativity. The more you use, the more you have."

"There's a world of difference between truth and facts. Facts can obscure the truth."

<u>Why does the caged bird in Maya Angelou's poem sing?</u>

"The caged bird in Maya Angelou's poem sings to express itself… Angelou's poem employs the metaphor in order to convey the idea that freedom is a natural state and knowledge of this fact cannot be undone by any amount of oppression or imprisonment."

Proverbs 3:5

Trust in the Lord with all thine heart, and lean not unto thine own understanding.

Proverbs 3:6

In all thy ways acknowledge him, and he shall direct thy paths.

CHAPTER 11

Power God gives us

In the natural world, we think of power as some form of force that we apply to achieve some objective. Such as the energy needed to move a car down a road at 60 miles per hour. The required power to run all the electrical items in a house. The type of energy is or can be express as in some form of mathematic formula.

In the spiritual world, power usually is accompanied by the term authority. Several well-known scriptures describe the states of the power given to Christians. Luke 10:19, Jesus has given us the power to overcome all the power of the enemy, and nothing shall harm us.

Luke 10:19 Behold, I give you power to tread on serpents and scorpions, and overall the power of the enemy: and nothing shall by any means hurt you.

Matthew 18:18 Verily I say unto you, Whatsoever ye shall bind on earth shall be bound in heaven: and whatsoever ye shall loose on earth shall be loosed in heaven.

Matthew 18:19 Again I say unto you, That if two of you shall agree on earth as touching anything that they shall ask, it shall be done for them of my father which is in heaven.

Acts 1:8 But ye shall receive power, after that the Holy Ghost is come upon you: and ye shall be witnesses unto me both in Jerusalem, and in all Judaea, and /Samaria, and unto the uttermost part of the earth.

But the core foundation for these given powers is "Christians have power and authority because they belong to Jesus who has all power and all authority.

There are some powers derived from spiritual gifts:

Word of Wisdom

World of Knowledge

Increase Faith

Gifts of Healing

Gift of Miracles

Prophecy

Discerning of Spirits

Divers Kind of Tongues

Interpretation of Tongues

There is a relationship between faith and power. It may be a direct relationship, an increase in faith results in an increase in power. Faith, the size of a mustard seed, can generate enough power to move a mountain.

Proverbs 2:6 For God giveth wisdom: out of his mouth cometh knowledge and understanding.

Proverbs 1:7 The fear of the Lord is the beginning of knowledge: but fools despise wisdom and instruction.

Proverbs 19:2 Also, that the soul be without knowledge, it is not good; and he that hasteth with feet sinneth.

Proverbs 18:15 The heart of the prudent getteth knowledge; and the ear of the wise seeketh knowledge.

Proverbs 15:14 The heart of him that hath understanding seeketh knowledge: but the mouth of fools feedeth on foolishness.

Proverbs 2:1 My son, if thou wilt receive my words, and hide my commandments with thee;

Proverbs 2:2 So that thou incline thine ear unto wisdom, and apply thine heart to understanding;

Proverbs 2:3 Yea, if thou criest after knowledge, and liftest up thy voice for understanding.

Proverbs 2:4 If thou sleekest her as silver, and searchest for her as for hid treasures;

Proverbs 2:5 Then shalt thou understand the fear of the Lord and find the knowledge of God.

Proverbs 2:6 For the Lord giveth wisdom: out of his mouth cometh knowledge and understanding.

Proverbs 2:7 He layeth up sound wisdom for the righteous: he is a buckler to them that walk uprightly.

Psalm 119:66 Teach me good judgment and knowledge: for I have believed thy commandments.

Proverbs 1:29 For that, they hated knowledge and did not choose the fear of the Lord.

Isaiah 11:2 And the Spirit of the Lord shall rest upon him, the Spirit of wisdom and understanding, the Spirit of counsel and might, the Spirit of knowledge and the fear of the Lord.

Keep reading; you will start to understand what has been going on around you to keep you down and bound. The Bible is like a coded book; as you keep reading, your mind starts to decipher what God wants you to know personally. And that goes for anyone else that begins reading the Bible. It is like a light goes on in your brain. God has given all of us the power (Dominion over everything) if we just let Him teach us.

Do you realize the power in this statement, Father God created us! The entire Earth God create with words, Man and every animal came into existence with words from God. God made us in His image. Do you realize the power that we have not yet developed? Just think about it.

Proverbs 12:16

A fool's wrath is presently known: but a prudent man covereth shame.

TEACH OUR CHILDREN

The Lord, thy God, tells us to teach our children and keep His commandments always that it will be well with our children forever and with us as parents. Before we can teach our children, we must have a spiritual mindset about them. For examples:

We do not own our kids; God tells us in Ezekiel 18:4 Behold, all souls are mine; as the soul of the father, so also the son is mine: the soul that sinneth, it shall die.

We will suffer great joy and sorrow because of our kids. God tells us in Proverbs 10:1 My son if sinners entice thee, consent thou not.

We must let go of our kids as they grow; God tells us in Genesis 2:24 Therefore shall a man leave his father and his mother, and shall cleave unto his wife; and they shall be one flesh.

God places the responsibility for teaching our children about Christianity on the parents. Not day-care centers, schoolteachers, or the village. Further, the successful accomplishment of this task will result in obtaining God's promise. If we teach our children to keep the Lord's commandments, it will be well for our children forever and with the parents a well. How will this task be achieved?

The Bible provides a list of things that we should teach our children. Many requirements are in Proverbs as well as other books like Ephesians and Colossians. Some of these requirements might seem contradictory, like, "spare rod, spoil the child, and do not provoke your child to wrath." But they are not really at odds with one another.

What is needed is for us to understand the role of "understanding and wisdom." We know all the requirements necessary to raise a child provided in the Bible (Child-like Christ). Wisdom offers the "how and how much" one needed for each child. To some degree, it is like baking a cake. We understand what ingredients are required. But wisdom tells us how much and when to mix the ingredients depending on the type of cake we are making.

Here is a partial list of appliable verses: KJV

Proverbs 1: 8 My son, hear the instruction of thy father, and forsake not the law of thy mother:

Proverbs 1:9 For they shall be an ornament of grace unto thy head, and chains about thy neck.

Proverbs 3:12 For whom the Lord loveth he correcteth; even as a father the son in whom he delighteth.

Proverbs 10:1 My son, if sinners entice thee, consent thou not.

Proverbs 13:24 He that spareth his rod hateth his son: but he that loveth him chasteneth him betimes.

Proverbs 22:6 Train up a child in the way he should go: and when he is old, he will not depart from it.

Proverbs 23:2 And put a knife to thy throat if thou be a man given to appetite.

(Proverbs 23:2) – It is not a real knife. It is telling you to bridle your tongue, refrain from too much talking, you may say something offensive.

Proverbs 31:26 She openeth her mouth with wisdom; and in her tongue is the law of kindness.

Proverbs 31:27 She looketh well to the ways of her household, and eateth not the bread of idleness.

Proverbs 31:28 Her children arise up, and call her blessed; her husband also, and he praiseth her.

Proverbs 31:29 Many daughters have done virtuously, but thou excellest them all.

Proverbs 31:30 Favour is deceitful, and beauty is vain: but a woman that feareth the Lord, she shall be praised.

Proverbs 31:31 Give her of the fruit of her hands; and let her own works praise her in the gates.

Exodus 20:12 Honour thy father and thy mother: that thy days may be long upon the land which the Lord thy God giveth thee.

How to treat All People:

1 Timothy 5:1 Rebuke not an elder, but intreat him as a father, and the younger men as brethren;

1 Timothy 5:2 The elder women as mothers; the younger as sisters with all purity.

1 Peter 4:8 And above all things have fervent charity among yourselves: for CHARITY SHALL COVER THE MULTITUDE OF SINS.

Colossians 3:20 Children, obey your parents in all things: for this is well-pleasing unto the Lord.

Colossians 3:21 Fathers, provoke not your children to anger, lest they be discouraged.

Ephesian 6:1 CHILDREN, obey your parents in the Lord: for this is right.

Today in our real world, look at all the violent hurricanes, tornadoes, turbulent storms, earthquakes, tsunamis, sinkholes, and uncontrollable fires across the earth. The atmosphere and land are feeling the evilness and poisonousness of the inhabitants on this earth.

This evilness is pouring into the churches; people are shot for no apparent reason while in church worshipping God. A gunman walks into the churches, Synagogues, and Holy Temples and shoots. Others are gun down in the street, run down by trucks, shot while sitting and enjoying a live concert. Is this an indication that the Lord thy God has moved his hands from us because of our wickedness?

We need to use social media more and appeal to the hearts of the people because they are a lot of broken souls there in the world that do not know of God's love.

Angry people; are generally upset with the world system; usually, they take their anger out on the innocent bystanders going about their daily routines.

We need more social and medical intervention to give help to these lost souls that need healing.

We need to integrate a lot more information into the complexity of learning, by not just giving pieces of the puzzle. But by combining the whole problem (teacher-student interaction), that provides the student with complete information. This way, students attain more knowledge and establish higher expectations for learning by integrating more details and concepts for all students to excel.

These new concepts of integrating more information will encourage the students to ask more questions and use more thinking techniques to attain and keep the knowledge that they have learned and not memorized.

Every aspect of learning (knowledge) is measurable by writing measurable learning objectives for your students.

Students genuinely are concern about their education but need to be shown how to retain learning and their knowledge of the information they have received.

God has made us teachers, and we are to teach our children.

The Bible says: Matthew 5:13 Ye are the salt of the earth: but if the salt have lost his savour, wherewith shall it be salted? It is thenceforth good for nothing, but to be cast out, and to be trodden under foot of men.

The Bible says: Matthew 5:14 Ye are the light of the world. A city that is set on an hill cannot be hid.

Matthew 5:16 Let your light so shine before men, that they may see your good works, and glorify your Father which is in heaven. If you pull Matthew 5:13, 5:14, and 5:16 apart: You are The

Salt of the Earth, You are The Light, Let Your Light Shine.

You know that Lord God put us here on earth as His seeds. Many people do not know their purpose.

Guess what? What salt gives flavor to; we need to provide more of that flavor to God's living word.

Biblical knowledge is a powerful weapon for improving the education of our children and building self-esteem.

While the Lord God is teaching, his seeds are learning, and we have a tremendous responsibility to make sure all children receive this teaching.

Remember, we are the salt of the earth.

The purpose of our gifts, like the Bible, say's in Ephesians 4:12 For the perfecting of the saints, for the work of the ministry, for the edifying of the body of Christ:

Ephesians 4:13 Till we all come in the unity of the Faith, and of the knowledge of the son of God, unto a perfect man, unto the measure of the stature of the fullness of Christ:

Note: We are the body of Christ; every day is a learning process. We are all the Lord God's children, and he loves us all, in the Bible, it says.

Psalms 45:17 I will make thy name to be remembered in all generations: therefore shall the people praise thee forever and ever.

Keep your eyes focused on God.

John 16:12 I have yet many things to say unto you, but ye cannot bear then now.

God gave us power; in Genesis, it tells us, God gave us dominion over everything. But we did not do right by this gift we received. We let sin into our lives and still do so today.

Man has not learned that God wants us to be knowledgeable God-fearing people, totally understanding the word.

CHAPTER 12

Gods Animals teach People

The funnies Team that lives on Mr. Hartman's Farm

Mr. Hartman is the owner of a farm in County Corners, located in Yellow Caw City. Mr. Hartman is not married and has no children, just his four (4) farm animals name Dreyfus the pig, Squat the hog, Moorse the goat, and Walter, the bird. They make a swell team; they are giddy and funny.

One Sunday afternoon, Mr. Patrick, the delivery man, was delivering some packages from Wiggly Jiggly grocery store, and Dreyfus and the others were eavesdropping on Mr. Hartman and Mr. Patrick's conversation.

Dreyfus - Did you hear what Mr. Patrick was telling Mr. Hartman about Fake Health foods?

Squat - Yes, what is Fake Health food?

Dreyfus - Mr. Patrick said it was food that had a large number of Lectins, which are a kind of protein that binds to sugar, and if you overeat, it can cause indigestion and gas.

Moorse - Maybe that's what my problem is because I have had a lot of gas lately.

Walter - Oh, be quiet, Moorse, you had gas since you been born, and you light up the place. Hee, Hee, because you eat everything you see.

Moorse - you do not do too badly yourself, Walter, eating Mr. Hartman's cheese he left on his plate on the patio last Sunday morning, tweet, tweet, tweet.

Moorse - What else did he say, Dreyfus?

Dreyfus - he talked about the vegetables Mr. Hartman should be eating for his health, like vegetables and fish, to help him cut down on his belly fat. Squat chimed in and said, and then he will never decide to eat us. Yes, let's encourage him to eat more vegetables and fish (Smile).

Dreyfus - I think Mr. Hartman is concern about his weight and his belly fat. I saw him looking in the mirror the other day, rubbing his belly, saying This Has to go. At the time, I didn't know what he meant by that (now we do).

Squat - Isn't Mr. Hartman a teacher at Quarter Berry Elementary School on Town Road…yes said Moorse.

Walter - I think it's time we talk to Mr. Hartman about suggesting a healthy food program for himself and all the children at his school. If he talks to the principal, Mr. Walpole, I think he'll agree!

Dreyfus - But Mr. Hart does not know we can speak, I thought we all were going to keep this a secret between us four (4), plus he does not know we can read and write either.

Dreyfus - Walter flies down to the basement; the window is open, take your carrier bag, and load it up with an envelope, pen, paper, and a stamp, Squat you can write the letter as follows, and Walter will mail as usual.

The Letter:

Dear Mr. Hartman,

As concerned citizens of the Town of County Corners, we would like you to be the spokesperson to speak with the principal at Quarter Berry Elementary School to start a health Food program. Our concern is the health situation around the country, with youth obesity on the rise.

As family members of the Town, we all felt you would be the best person for this petition. We know you will not let us down, and we thank you in advance!

Respectfully,

Concern parents of County Corners, Yellow Caw City

Walter - I mailed the letter, Mr. Hartman should receive it tomorrow at the latest.

Dreyfus - Are we all in favor that keeping our secret is a wise thing to do? It's unanimous, and we are all in agreement (Yay)!

Moorse - You know Squat, if Mr. Hartman gets a dog that could live in the house, we would be privy to more information while he's on the phone, plus when he has a lot of company, we need to find a dog and tell the dog our plan sounds great yappy do, this may work!

Mr. Hartman spoke with the Principal, Mr. Walpole, on the concern of the family members of the Town. In turn, Mr. Walpole talked to the Superintendent of the school, Mr. Kirby. Mr. Kirby thought it was a great idea to start a health food program and recommended the application be started at once and in place within two weeks. There Motto: "HEALTHY BALANCE DIETS MAKES FOR HEALTHIER AND WISER CHILDREN"

The funnies team on the farm said, "When you stand for something, it means something" And when you can read and write, "You have mastered the fight, even the Animals have learned this game."

CHAPTER 13

The Next Generation

Oh God, how do we make this all clear to the next generation of youth? How can they comprehend if the words of Lord God are not being spoken or taught in their homes?

How do the youth find their identity in the Lord God? How can we get the youth back to knowing the Lord God?

The answer might be related to their past experiences; first, you need to refer to their struggles and doubts, which lead them away from God in the first place!

The Bible is not easy to read for understanding and could be very confusing.

That's why, when a young child is first guided by his or her parents to start the reading. They are to be led in Prayer, Lord, God gives me wisdom and understanding to read your Word in this Bible with clarity. And let every scripture provide you with clarity.

Psalm 25:12 What man is he that feareth the Lord? Him shall he teach in the way that he shall choose.

Deuteronomy 6:6 And these words, which I command thee this day, shall be in thine heart.

Deuteronomy 6:7 And thou shalt teach them diligently unto thy children, and shalt talk of them when thou sitteth in thine house, and when thou walkest by the way, and when thou liest down, and when thou risest up.

Bible Knowledge

Since you do not have your Bible in front of you, while reading this, I'm going to type each verse out.

Proverbs 2:6 For the Lord giveth wisdom: out of his mouth cometh knowledge and understanding.

Proverbs 1:7 The fear of the Lord is the beginning of knowledge: but fools despise wisdom and instructions.

Proverbs 19:2 Also, that the soul be without knowledge, it is not good; and he that hasteth with his feet Sinneth.

Proverbs 18:15 The heart of the prudent getteth knowledge; and the ear of the wise seeketh knowledge.

Proverbs 15:14 The heart of him that hath understanding seeketh knowledge: but the mouth of fools feedeth on foolishness.

Proverbs 2:1 My son, if thou wilt receive my words, and hide my commandments with thee, then shalt thou understand the fear of the Lord and find the knowledge of God.

Proverbs 2:2 So that thou incline thine ear unto wisdom, and apply thine heart to understanding.

Proverbs 2:3 Yea, if thou criest after knowledge, and liftest up thy voice for UNDERSTANDING.

Proverbs 2:4 If thou sleekest her as silver, and searchest for her as for hid treasures.

Proverbs 2:5 shalt thou understand the fear of the Lord, and find knowledge of God.

Proverbs 2:6 For the Lord giveth wisdom: out of his mouth cometh knowledge and understanding.

Proverbs: 2:7 He layeth up sound wisdom for the righteous: he is a buckler to them that walk uprightly.

EPILOGUE

We need to walk by Faith, not by sight, and we need to do all that we do in love. We need to humble ourselves before God and ask Him for wisdom in our daily journey through life.

Deuteronomy Chapter 11:1 (KJV)

Therefore thou shall love the Lord thy God, and keep his charge, and his statutes, and his judgments, and his commandments, always.

That Word Always, Means for Forever! Deuteronomy Chapter 11:2 (KJV)

And know ye this day: for I speak not with your children which have not seen the chastisement of the Lord your God, his greatness, his mighty hand, and his stretched out arm.

We have a grave responsibility as parents to teach our children the words of God, that they grow in wisdom and understand of God's Word and pass God's Word from generation to generation.

Proverbs 22:6 (KJV)

Train up a child in the way he should go, and when he is old, he will not depart from it.

Remember, in life, manipulation is injustice. It's a unique way of impeding the progress of the people, remove your blinders. Stand back to see what's taking place.

It takes enormous strength to walk away and hold your tongue in a fight. You cannot affect change if you are dead. The violence in the street must stop. Your consciousness is never going to be activated if you immediately respond to a violent situation. There is an evil spirit electrifying real injustice to the extinction of humankind.

When you have violence in the streets anywhere, it has been orchestrated by one person mostly to get the crowd riled up. The ultimate weapon is the action of a person that consciously grasps the right time to say something negative in a group of people.

That is the evil external guidance that starts fights, burns storefronts, and buildings down, plus gets other people killed.

There is a world of unhappy people out in the streets today that is looking for legitimate answers and justice. Without provocation, people are out on the roads for truth and answers.

The younger generation is no longer going to stand by and be the invisible generation.

It is sadly evident that our justice system is suffering a hiccup, and they need to get on the ball to address exiting problems in the streets, intolerance, and bias related to police and public safety. To extinguish a fire, you use water. To calm people down, you need to answer their questions and not make light of any issues. It can be lethal when you don't keep people informed. You are igniting mental anguish along the way in a crowd of people that causes anxiety, behavioral disorder, and the crumbling of order within a massive group of people.

Remember, knowledge and poverty exist, but prosperity is embarking on the injustice that the people themselves are feeling.

Someone will perish within the conversions of the deceit of the police reporting when you had someone filming the entire incident. If you cannot change some of the government and police beliefs, it is insane to think they can change the minds of the people.

The illusion has shown its face, the people saw a cover-up taking place, and it has happened more than once. And the government and police departments have not adequately addressed this problem of racial indiscretions, a gentle way of saying prejudice does exist.

The meaning of this outcry of the people in the streets and all over the world is because they can see firsthand via social media what transpired. And what the government system lets happen.

They are converging on society through social media platforms, that everything can go public in honesty to electrify and exploit the acknowledgment of the killings and injustice. To embellish over the news media that this is not a T.V. show, it was a live killing of an individual.

Thank God for the advanced technology of cell phones, to be able to take pictures and record everything and immediately put it on the airways. That looks like legal documentation.

If it was not for this new technology a lot of miss justice would not be up in the face of people for real. Certain conditions in life have shown their face. And those of society can no longer push dirty things up under the rugs any long.

Technology pat yourself on the back, it is the new technology that will make you wiser, everything will be clear

So now I say, we need to address our words without starting a fire through insinuations.

The Moment you looked back in your life if you digress a little, you will have to realize God has been with you on your journey.

Let's just say the sharpest tool in the shed is God I am glad He is with us all the time! AMEN!

God is the pilot and I am the passenger..don't get it twisted! So, we can go non-stop! (SMILE)

About The Author

Virginia Edge is the author of The Moment I Looked Back. It's interesting how we always want to look back over our lives. We cannot change the past, but we sure can change our future with all of God's help. The author states God loves to hear from us every day. God wants us to know His word and learn of Him in Jesus's Name.

She is a Registered Nurse, now retired for 23 years, born in New York. The oldest girl of 3 children. She is married to Theron Edge for 42 years.

They have 3 Children,7 Grandchildren,3 Great- Grandchildren, and one dog named Maxis. She has a great love for her family and her little Maxis.

She firmly believes that parents are to teach their children of God's Word and explain why God's Word is essential in their lives. Virginia has been a sponsor for children at World Vision, building a better world for children, for the past 22 years, since

06/04/1999.

If you are ever interested in sponsoring a child from any part of the world, you can write or call World Vision, or go to their website.

World Vision, Inc./Love2Learn P.O.Box 9716
Federal Way, WA 98063
Phone # 1-888-511-6548/ 1-888-511-6534
Donation: (World Vision.org.)

She also donates to the Mercy Ship program that follows the 2000-year old model of Jesus to provide hope and healing to the world's forgotten poor.

For 40 years, Mercy Ship has offered medical services across the globe, giving confidence to millions who struggle to survive and have limited or no access to healthcare. The Mercy Ship serves all people without regard for race, gender, or religion.

Donation: (MercyShip.org)
MercyShips P.O.Box 1930
Garden Valley, TX 75771-1930

Her saying is, always be a blessing to someone else. Life's a recipe that can be found in any Bible because God (Jesus) never changes.

God Bless and Much Love in Jesus's Name!

The Moment I Looked Back

Outline/Synopsis

We are all human beings born into sin. Into a life of the unknown. We learn to integrate all information by Faith as we grow. We continue to look back at every moment in our lives for understanding and meaning.

1. We need the understanding to get meaning of our existence.

    a. What is your identity and who do we identify with?

    b. Why do we need guidance in God's word?

    c. How do we learn of God through His word?

2. Why do we need to understand God's word for growth in our life?

    a. Equality recognizes color blindness man has problems.

    b. Education and knowledge open our eyes and improves understanding.

    c. Our voices are invisible because we do not speak what we feel and understand.

3. We need to learn and become more knowledgeable of
   God's word for inner growth.

   a. God's power and understanding are what we need.

   b. Understanding is our responsibility in life.

   c. Wisdom and understanding help to integrate all the
      pieces in the puzzle of life.